Whispers of the Heart

A Collection of Poems
That Will
Serenade You with Every Verse

Faye Marks

Copyright © 2024 Markey Writing Academy

WHISPERS OF THE HEART

First published by Markey Writing Academy 2024

Find us on Facebook @KellyMarkeyAuthor, Instagram @Author_Kelly_Markey and LinkedIn @kellymarkey

Paperback ISBN: 978-1-7636837-1-6

E-Book ISBN: 978-1-7636837-2-3

Markey Writing Academy and the author of this book have asserted their rights under the Copyright, Designs and Patents Act 1988 to be identified as the author of this work. The information in this book is based on the author's experiences and opinions. The publisher specifically disclaims responsibility for any adverse consequences which may result from use of the information contained herein. Permission to use information has been sought by the author. Any breaches will be rectified in further editions of the book.

All rights reserved. No part of this publication may be reproduced, stored in or introduced into a retrieval system, or transmitted in any form, or by any means (electronic, mechanical, photocopying, recording or otherwise) without the prior written permission of the author. Any person who does any unauthorised act in relation to this publication may be liable to criminal prosecution and civil claims for damages. Enquiries should be made to the publisher.

Cover Design: Markey Writing Academy
Cover Image Graphic: Lizzie Ostermann
Layout: Markey Writing Academy
Typesetting: Markey Writing Academy

Markey Writing Academy
Central Coast New South Wales,
Australia 2250

www.kellymarkey.com

DEDICATION

This book is dedicated to my online support group and my Monday afternoon women's Bible study class. They have listened to me, been encouraging me, helping me to open up, and to be able to share and encourage others.

I have learned so much from both groups and I thank them for what they have done for me. I have also gained some lasting friendships.

I would also like to dedicate this book to all the people everywhere who are struggling. Not only with mental health or grief, but also health, fear, hopelessness, etc. May you all find the peace you need.

TABLE OF CONTENTS

FOREWORD 1
PREFACE 3
INTRODUCTION 5
DEPRESSION 7
    ANXIETY 8
    BE HAPPY 9
    BEING THERE 10
    CHEERFUL 12
    CLAP YOUR HANDS 13
    CONFUSION 14
    DISTRACTED 16
    DETERMINED 18
    DREARY DAY 19
    EMOTIONS 20
    FALLING 22
    FEELING THIS WAY 24
    FIGHTING 25
    FILLING TIME 26
    FIND THE GOOD 27
    GOING DOWN 29
    GOING OUT 30
    GRAY WEATHER 32
    HELP ME 33
    IS IT TRUE 34
    JUDGEMENTS 36
    LIFE 37
    LUCKY? 38
    MOTIVATION 39
    NOT GOOD 41
    NOT REAL 42
    NOT RIGHT 43
    PANIC 44
    PROBLEMS? 45
    SHAME AND GUILT 46
    SLEEP 47
    SO DIM 49
    SO DOWN TODAY 51
    SO EMOTIONAL 52
    SO MUCH TO BE DONE 54
    SO TIRED 55

SPRING 56
THE SUN.. 57
TIRED... 58
TOO GOOD TO BE TRUE... 59
UNAWARE... 60
UP AND DOWN.. 61
VISITING MY DAUGHTER 62
WHAT'S GOING ON... 63
WHERE DO I GO?.. 64
WHY 66
WHY CAN'T I CRY?.. 67
WHY DO I CRY? 68
WHY IS IT?.. 70
WITH YOU 71

MY DAUGHTER'S POEMS 72

THAT DAY ON THE PLAYGROUND 73
THREAD OF HOPE... 75

GRIEF... 77

DECORATING THE TREE 80
NEW YEARS DAY 82
GONE SO LONG... 83
STRUGGLE 84
FORGIVE ME... 85
MIXED FEELINGS 87
MEMORIES.. 88
FUNERAL 90
GRIEF 92
MISSING HIM.. 94
AWOKE 96
MISS YOU MORE 98
TOO MUCH... 100
CHRISTMASTIME IS HERE 102
TIME.. 103
THE OTHER NIGHT... 105
CARRY ON 106
DO YOU STILL LOVE ME? 108
MISS YOU TODAY 109

A NEW JOURNEY 110

WHAT TO DO 111
DEPRESSED... 113
DEPRESSION IN THE BIBLE 115

DISCUSSION	116
TOO ANXIOUS	118
PATIENCE	121
THINKING	122
WAITING	124

MISCELLANEOUS 125

A LOVING PRAYER	126
WHEN WORDS FALL SHORT	127
UNCONDITIONAL	128
GRAND DAUGHTER'S POEM	129

PEOPLE 130

TO JEFF	131
LOIS	132
LORRAINE	133
PASTOR APPRECIATION	134
RED	136
RUTH AND MARSHALL	137
TERRI	139

VARIOUS THOUGHTS 140

ADDICTION	141
JOURNEY	143
THE SEASONS	144
TIME	146
MY HOPE	147
MY BELIEFS	149
GONE	153
THE HOLY TRINITY	154
REJOICE	156
GOD IS GREAT	157

ODDS AND ENDS 158

CLASS REUNION	160
FIREFLIES	162
FIREWORKS	163
FOOTBALL	164
PORTA-POTTY	165

ABOUT THE AUTHOR 166

ACKNOWLEDGEMENTS 169

Faye Marks

FOREWORD

In a world often filled with the noise of daily life, the quiet moments of grief and loss can feel both overwhelming and isolating. "Whispers of the Heart" is a testament to the power of words to heal, connect, and transcend time. This captivating book, written by Faye Marks, my dearest friend who truly is a remarkable one-of-a-kind woman. This collection is more than just poetry - it is her legacy, a heartfelt offering to her family and future generations.

These poems were born from a place of deep sorrow, penned in the wake of the loss of her beloved husband. Through each word, she confronted her grief, found solace in the act of creation, and allowed her pain to bloom into something beautiful. But this book is not solely about her own journey. It is her gift to all those who have struggled with grief, mental health, and the haunting thoughts of suicide. Her hope is that these poems will bring comfort, understanding, and a sense of companionship to those who feel alone in their struggles.

As a woman of fervent dedicated faith, Faye's writing is deeply rooted in the love and promises of God. She found strength in Scripture during her darkest moments, and it is her prayer that others might find the same. One verse that I'd like to share with you that has helped many through this journey is from the book of Psalms:

* "The Lord is close to the broken-hearted and saves those who are crushed in spirit." * Psalm 34:18 (NIV).

In addition to the poems, this book carries a special piece of art, a drawing of a heart on the cover created by her granddaughter. It is a symbol of the love that has bound their family through generations, a love that transcends time, loss, and grief. This heart serves as a visual reminder that even through the pain, love remains at the centre - steady, healing, infinite, unconditional and eternal.

As you open this book, I invite you to fully open your mind and your heart as well. Whatever wounds you carry from the storms of life - whether from grief, loss, mental struggles, or simply the weariness of life's peaks and valleys can bring - know that you are not alone. These words are a reminder that healing is possible, and love is always present, even when it feels distant.

Allow yourself to be fully aware, to feel, to heal, and to know that you are loved beyond measure, no matter what you are going through. May these beautifully written poems be a comforting hand, guiding you to peace and reminding you that God's love, like the love woven into these pages, is unfailing.

"Whispers of the Heart" is a reminder that even in our darkest hours, there is light and hope to be found. This collection is filled with the wisdom, love, and resilience that only a long life well-lived can offer. May her words inspire, heal, and serve as a lasting memory of her family, and as a beacon of hope for others around the world.

In reading this, you are not just experiencing poetry - you are witnessing the strength of the human spirit and the enduring power of love.

Nadene Joy
CEO of Nadene Joy Consulting Inc.
www.NadeneJoy.com

PREFACE

This book is a continuation of my first book, *"Poems from the Heart."* They are written for you and anyone else who is struggling with any kind of mental health issue, grief, or another kind of problem. They are meant to give you hope that things will get better and let you know you are not alone.

The poems mostly concern my depression and grief. After sharing some of my poems with other people, I received a lot of positive feedback. My support group said they were so identifiable with their situations. It was suggested that I should put them in a book so others could read and benefit from them.

After publishing my first book, many people told me how much it had helped them or a friend they knew. My daughter just recently gave my book to a woman who had just lost her husband. After reading it, she returned and told my daughter that it had really helped her. Hearing that just made my day!

That is the reason for both my books. I want people in situations like mine to be inspired and encouraged by them. I want to give them hope for a better tomorrow, and maybe they will turn around and help someone else. If my poems can accomplish this, then I will publish them. If just one person can be helped by them, it will be worth it.

As stated before, the poems are my feelings written in poetry form. Some of them are cheery, some are sad.

Some are intertwined with my belief in God. They are all the innermost feelings I have experienced throughout my life.

I want you to know there is someone who does care and understands you. They are out there just waiting to help you. I am with you. You are not alone.

> These poems have given me great relief
> In my troubles, in my grief
> As you read the words written here
> May you feel peace and have no fear
> ---*fem*

INTRODUCTION

This book is published for you and anyone else who can benefit from the words and meanings of my poems. It is meant to help you deal with any problems you might have. This book is full of poems that were inspired by my experiences with long-time depression and grief from the loss of my husband a little over three years ago. I kept my depression a secret for many, many years, thinking people would think less of me if they knew. I "wore a mask" pretending things were great when I had problems. It was not until my first book came out that anyone knew about my depression. It was a scary thing to do, but I wanted to help others who felt the same way I did. I wanted to be free of all the hiding, pretending, and stress that came from not opening up.

My poems are a sincere expression of my true feelings, and I believe others can relate to them as well. I received positive responses from my first book, and I hope to have a similar experience with this one. Knowing that these poems made people contemplate, connect with their own experiences, and helped them in their struggles, gave me strength I needed.

Depression is something that many people experience occasionally. For some, like me, it can be a chronic condition that requires ongoing management. Coping with the loss of a loved one, such as my husband, can make it even more challenging to deal with.

I hope that through these poems, you will come to understand that it's not just you who experiences these kinds of problems. This book is intended to offer help, encouragement, and inspiration to you. I believe that dealing with these challenges has made me stronger, and I hope the same for you.

Love to all!

DEPRESSION

Depression is something so many people have once or twice in their lifetime. For others, they live with it for the rest of their lives. The feelings and moods go up and down, back and forth. These poems are my experiences of those ups and downs.

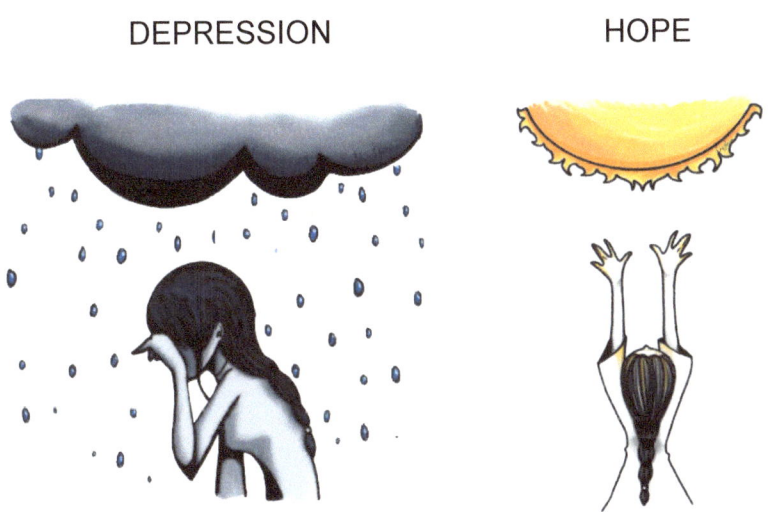

Illustrated by Lizzie Ostermann

ANXIETY

So much anxiety I want to cry
My stomach full of butterflies
So many events are coming up
I don't know when it will stop

Trips, appointments and other things
All this anxiety they bring
What can I do to get by
To get rid of these butterflies

I think too much about things
What the events might bring
I need to keep myself in the day
I don't think there's another way

Try to keep your mind in the now
Try to keep busy somehow
Don't let the worry take over you
There is so much in life waiting for you
---fem

BE HAPPY

The elderly are to be happy each day
That's what I had heard someone say
Is it possible for this to happen
Especially if you have depression

Your feelings go up and down each day
How can your happiness stay
When people ask how you are doing
I'm ok, I'm fine is the answer I'm giving

Am I fooling myself or them
Is my mask on again
How can I let them know the truth
When I've done this since my youth

I can tell them that I am fine
But are those feelings really mine
I need to get my mood changed around
So more happiness can be found

Be truthful to those who ask
Which for me is quite a task
Maybe with help of family and friends
All my dishonesty will end

They could help me in some way
To feel better day by day
So get on with your life, do it for you
You can change and be happy too

---fem

BEING THERE

I don't want to be here
My thoughts are not clear
What is the reason I feel this way
I am hoping these thoughts go away

There's so much to do
And loving people too
Life is worth living
So keep on believing

Find for yourself a little joy
Try to do this and don't avoid
Never ever give up
Please, please don't stop

---fem

CHEERFUL

I was happy and cheerful today
It felt so good to be that way
The sun was warm and bright
It was good to see all that light

Is it because it's the first day of spring
Is that why it was happening
Everyone seemed to be so friendly
And my life didn't feel so empty

It was a day that I enjoyed
And bad feelings I could avoid
The day went by way too fast
And soon it will be in the past

Yes, I was happy today
Please don't take that feeling away
I want every day to be like this
There are so many that I've missed

---fem

CLAP YOUR HANDS

If you're happy and you know it clap your hands
There is so much that this world demands
But if depression overtakes you
There are things that you can do

Though everything you try
Is so hard it makes you cry
If you finally get out of bed
Trying to face the day ahead

If you call a friend in need
That will also help indeed
If you go outside to take a walk
Or to someone you can talk

If you finally do some dishes
Or a chore that you've been wishing
There still is hope for you
And hope for me too

Each little step that you take
Is time to celebrate
We're with you all the while
And we try to make you smile

If you're a little happier today
Than you were yesterday
It's time for all of us
To clap our hands

---*fem*

CONFUSION

So much going around in my head
Spinning around, I can't go to bed
All this thinking is it real
So confused with what I feel

How can I sort it all out
So many things to think about
All these things going around in my head
What I thought, what was said

All mixed up I can't figure them out
What is this all about
Everything mixing together inside
No place to go no place to hide

So many thoughts what do I do
Is my thinking wrong or true
All these things I am thinking about
How do I sort them all out

This all makes me feel trapped
Locked in a place where I can't get back
My anxiety is going up
How do I make all of this stop

All this makes me want to shout
I need to figure all of this out
I need to make my head clear
From all the things that I fear

---fem

DISTRACTED

I get distracted so much of the time
I start one thing and then I find
Something else gets my attention
Happening so many times to mention

I start doing something at my own pace
When I am there a distraction takes place
When it happens my mind turns to that
But then when I start distraction is back

Something else has caught my eye
I start doing that not knowing why
This keeps going around and around
I've finished nothing I have found

What I need to do is concentrate
So when I get done it's not too late
I don't like leaving things half done
I want to finish something, just one

How can I keep my mind on one thing
To finish before my mind starts to swing
How can I keep it under control
Getting things done is my goal

How to stop my mind from racing
This is a problem I am facing
To get one thing done before another
Would be a feeling like no other

I am starting another task
Why isn't the other one done I ask
Around and around I go
Will it stop? I don't know

---fem

DETERMINED

It's been a week and I'm still feeling good
I hope it stays; I wish it would
But I am always afraid the ball will drop
And all my happiness will stop

This is always in the back of my mind
As it has happened so many times
Nothing good ever seems to stay
My life has always been that way

I need to change my thoughts of this
I am determined not to miss
All the happiness that lies ahead
And to ignore the bad with no tears shed

It will be hard, quite a challenge in fact
But it's all in the way I react
Don't be afraid of the good things to be
But be aware bad things could happen to me

But don't let it get out of hand
Be determined and take a stand
This life is oh so very short
Don't let your world fall apart
---fem

DREARY DAY

Today is another dreary day
We've had so many days that way
The rain is falling and then it snows
What will tomorrow be, who knows

I'm not able to open the doors
It's too cold and damp for sure
The migrated birds are chirping outside
But I can't hear them from the inside

I want to go out and get some sun
To walk in the yard - what needs to be done
There is so much work to do
I want to get at it and finish it too

But right now, I'll have to wait
For cheery days, who knows the date
Maybe then I'll feel better again
When the sun shines though I don't know when

This all affects how I feel
I know that these feelings are very real
For the sun and warm days, I can't wait
It will then be a time to celebrate
---fem

EMOTIONS

Lately I have been so emotional
I cry about things both big and small
Good things that happen, things that are sad
All make me cry which makes me mad

Tears start flowing all of a sudden
I don't want this to always happen
I think too much about lots of things
Then a lot of sadness it brings

When good things happen, I turn it around
There is no happiness to be found
What can I do to stop all of this
Just being me is what I miss

I used to be happy so much of the time
I felt so good, I felt so fine
But now I feel down and out you see
This isn't what I want for me

I don't want to cry all the time
Just a few would be perfectly fine
The happy moments I'd like to savor
And enjoy them and not waiver

What in the world can I do
Has this ever happened to you?
I need to get myself turned around
So less crying can be found

My emotions are so many right now
I want them to go but I don't know how
I want all the crying to stop
So happy will be at the top
---fem

FALLING

I feel so very down today
Why do I feel this way
Yesterday I felt just fine
Like the world could be mine

So happy I was yesterday
Why can't that feeling stay
I have a headache instead
My thoughts are racing in my head

They won't come out though I try
They spin around and I cry
I lose my balance and fall to the ground
I can't get up or make a sound

I'm frozen I can't move at all
No one would hear me if I could call
I try to get up but I'm slipping
Like a statue that is tipping

Oh what will happen to me
No help for me can I see
People keep passing me by
I still can't move, so hard I try

Then someone reaches for my hand
To help me up, to help me stand
It's so hard to move my hand
Will I slip and fall again

But I am determined, so again I try
He holds me close and then I cry
For I am standing up again
And on the ground I do not land

He has helped me up somehow
I am feeling better now
I now call this man my friend
I know If I fall he'll help me up again
---fem

FEELING THIS WAY

Why do I feel this way
It wasn't really a bad day
But now I am all stressed out
What is this feeling all about

My interests are making me bored
Things undone that can't be ignored
Nothing seems to be working right
How will I get to sleep tonight

So much going on in my head
And anxious feelings go unsaid
How can I settle myself down
There is no one but me around

I feel my head is starting to shrink
I feel like I am starting to sink
How can I get afloat
I can't swim, there is no boat

I need to stop thinking this way
To think of the good from today
Tomorrow will be brand new
Maybe I'll feel better too
---fem

FIGHTING

I feel this depression coming on
But I don't want it to get me down
I'm fighting it as hard as I can
But I don't know where my mind will land

Why does this have to be
Why does this come over me
How can I get it to quit
I want to keep going in spite of it

Just tell me what I can do
To help myself from feeling blue
It's always a struggle to get it to stop
I need to get my feelings up

The fight seems to be wearing me out
I'm tired of this there is no doubt
I need the answers now, right now
To chase this depression away somehow

---fem

FILLING TIME

What do you do to keep busy
For some people it is really easy
For others they just don't know
They wonder what or where to go

Keeping busy makes days go faster
Is that what you are after
You need to find what you enjoy
Not just something to fill your time

Whether you volunteer or stay home
All this time is your own
Do something that interests you
But don't forget to see people too

Keep looking for what you need
When you find it you will see
You will enjoy your life more
So much more than you did before

It will give you more fulfillment
And your time will be well spent
Keep looking and don't give up
Keep your light shining and don't stop
---fem

FIND THE GOOD

This world may seem troubled right now
You wonder if it will get better somehow
You may also feel really bad
There are things that make you so sad

Things in your life might happen
That you think can never worsen
You feel nothing ever goes right
It seems you are losing the fight

There are good things out there
Though you can't find them anywhere
You may even wonder why
Why should you even try

There is good all around you
Finding it may be hard to do
But there is hope for us all
Even in the times you fall

Look very hard and you will find
There is someone who is kind
There is someone out there
Someone who truly cares

Good is intertwined with the bad
But it is always there to be had
Keep the good above all
You'll feel better overall

Concentrate on good things today
Chase those negative things away
There is hope in all you do
Find it now it's good for you

Remember you are not alone
These feelings aren't just your own
Everyone has something discouraging
You just need some encouraging

We all have faith in you
The same faith you should have too
Find the good in every day
You'll be happier this way
---*fem*

GOING DOWN

I can feel myself going down
Down to a place I won't be found
All this negativity in my mind
My way back up, will I find?

What can I do, what brought this on
All my positive feelings are gone
Why am I here, what is my purpose
Can't figure out why I feel so hopeless

I feel like there is no one who cares
I get no attention from anywhere
It seems that I'm invisible to them
Will they ever see me? Tell me when

Why do I keep going unnoticed, why
Why do people keep passing me by
What is this thing, why am I missed
It makes me wonder if I really exist

I keep going down more and more
I have fallen below the floor
I'm in a hole and can't get out
No one hears me when I shout

Will these feelings and thoughts ever stop
Is there a way to pick myself up
Where can I go what can I do
To keep myself from feeling so blue

---fem

GOING OUT

I want to go out but I can't
I want to see people but I can't
What can I do to get fresh air
My feet are in concrete, not there

I want to stay home all the time
These are feelings that are mine
It gets so lonely when you're alone
I would be happier if I could go

How can I get myself out
Please tell me what it's all about
Trying to get out is so hard
I feel all my doors are barred
---fem

Support groups can be encouraging and so much help. This is a poem inspired by my support group and how I feel about them.

GRAY WEATHER

It is such a dreary day
It's raining and the clouds are gray
It is good for growing food
But it simply changes my mood

Why does it have such an effect
On how we feel and react
This is something that I wonder
It's like a spell it puts me under

Do you ever feel this way
As I do on this dreary day
If you do let's help each other
Share our thoughts with one another

We can do it if we stick together
We can do it no matter the weather
We can fight against it all
We'll pick you up if you fall

Together we can thrive through this
Together we just cannot miss
So, let's get started with this plan
Holding on to each other's hand
---fem

HELP ME

Help me! Help me! Everything is going wrong
All the things I try seem to take so long
Completion is something I do not see
Nothing is working for me

The problems are making me upset
The more there are the more irritable I get
My head is whirling around inside
Is there somewhere I can hide

In my stomach I feel butterflies
More and more my anxieties rise
There's so much that I want to do
But things get in the way too

I spend so much time fixing things
But more problems that all brings
My head is now spinning so fast
How long will these feelings last

There doesn't seem to be an end
So much time on this I spend
I just want to scream and shout
My nerves are shot there is no doubt

I need to stay calm and quiet down
And get rid of this big frown
I try but when I look around
There are more problems to be found

---*fem*

IS IT TRUE

My depression keeps me thinking
Of the bad things I am seeing
It doesn't let the good things in
It doesn't feel that I can win

I'm so tired of all of this
And all the things that I miss
They tell me God will help me
Is it really true for me

They say that He loves me
And from all sin He'll set me free
That he will give me comfort and peace
His guidance will never cease

This sounds so good but can it be
He will be here to strengthen me
So full of sadness and grief
Can He really give me relief

I do have faith and believe
Is that enough for me
Or do my doubts overtake
Will God forgive all my mistakes

I need to give all my problems to Him
In order for me to really win
He is waiting for me too
Please tell me what to do

Can I pray so He will hear
Can I really feel Him near
I am hoping this will be
Something I will be able to see

All the goodness and mercy He gives
And the wonderful world in which I live
Please make me strong so I can be
With Him in eternity

---fem

JUDGEMENTS

The way I talk, the way I feel
The way I walk, what's the big deal
Judgements are so hard to take
They can be cruel and make you shake

Some stay with us for a short time
Others are always in your mind
You try to forget them but you can't
You can always hear their chant

Many times you will be
Afraid to do things, they'll see
Many times you will stay inside
And you just want to hide

No peace is there hearing them say
All these things day after day
I don't think they really know
How it really hurts me so

How can I make them see
All I want is to be me
Not the clone of them, not me
Is this how the world should be

The person I want to be
Is someone who can be free
To make my thoughts all my own
and not feel so all alone

---*fem*

LIFE

Life can be wonderful
But so uncontrollable
No matter what you get
You have to deal with it

Some have no worries or fears
Some have so many they can't think clear
Some go on happy day after day
Some people just can't think that way

Whatever your problem, good or bad
You need to cope with what you have
So many or so little that you've been given
Life goes on and you need to keep living

Take care of yourself don't be afraid
Ask someone to give you aid
You can make it through life too
No matter what it's given you
---*fem*

LUCKY?

Can you be lucky to have depression
Sometimes this is what I envision
It's so difficult to control but yet
I wouldn't be me if I didn't have it

So many people that I meet
Through this struggle that I keep
I wouldn't have met them otherwise
Such good people who are so wise

They encourage you and help you
Cheer your accomplishments too
They help you when you're down
And help your feelings turn around

So many friends I have made
Through the caring that they gave
My life has changed because of them
The ones I hope will call me friend

So thank you for giving me
These good things that I see
Thank you for what I've been given
People who make life worth living

----fem

MOTIVATION

My sleep is going back to where it was
I just don't know what is the cause
There is something I just can't see
Why again is it happening to me

I feel better otherwise
Or is it just a disguise
Is it motivation I don't have
Is my head just cut in half

Still having problems paying the bills
I just don't seem to have the will
I always seem to procrastinate
With things that really shouldn't wait

What is the answer to all of this
What is the something that I miss
I need the answer so I know
How far will all of this really go

---fem

NOT GOOD

I just don't have that motivation
So tired of procrastination
I can't seem to get things done
Tell me am I the only one?

I start to do a lot of things
But irritability it brings
My feelings seem to have gone away
There's nothing there throughout the day

Nothing seems to work when I try
I feel like I'm barely getting by
There are things I have enjoyed
Now they are getting me annoyed

I feel like an empty shell
My concentration is starting to fail
I get distracted all the time
My mind keeps dragging behind

Doing things takes so much effort
I'm tired before I even start
So many things I need to do
Are just sitting there waiting too

How do I get out of this funk
My mind is full of so much junk
I cannot keep going on this way
Will tomorrow be better than today

---fem

NOT REAL

I heard some people say
In a very dramatic way
Mental illness is not real
It's just people making a big deal

But you and I know
This is not so
Every day is a struggle for us
To stay ahead of it we must

We keep trying day after day
To make those negative things go away
This is very tiring, of course
Then it comes back even worse

We need to get the word out
This is real there is no doubt
Try to change their misled minds
Maybe a change you will find

Depression is hard enough
What are people thinking of
If we put them in our shoes
What do you think they would do?
---fem

NOT RIGHT

Why can't I do anything right
Though I try with all my might
Why can't I be someone who
People like what I do

Everything I do goes wrong
I just don't know where I belong
I can't take all this anxiety
That is always filling me

Afraid to be seen, afraid to speak
Afraid to have what I seek
Why can't I be like others
And get to see what life offers

I feel I am all by myself
Without a friend, without help
In a space that feels so bad
That is dark and keeps me sad

All my life I've been like this
And think of all the things I miss
The feeling that no one cares
The feeling that no one knows I'm there

When I get the chance to be
The person I want them to see
My mind goes blank and I forget
All is gone and then I fret

Why can't I do anything right
This in me do I fight
But I seem to fail each time
Why does this feeling have to be mine
---fem

PANIC

I'm all alone, I am upset
How much worse can it get
I pace the floor back and forth
Things in my head I cannot sort

I'm nervous, I'm not feeling well
Is there someone I can tell
Calm down, calm down
I need to calm down

But this is not working for me
I'm getting worse, it can't be
I can't breathe, I can't breathe
What is happening to me

Oh no it's a panic attack
I need to get my breath back
I'm afraid so afraid, what can I do
I feel like I am turning blue

Try to take a deep breath now
How can I do that, how
I need to relax, can I do it
I think I really need to sit

I can take one breath so far
Then another but it is hard
Oh, it is starting to go away
Panic attacks happen that way

They are very hard to control
No more attacks is my goal
I do not want this to repeat
This is something I will defeat

---fem

PROBLEMS?

Is your problem big or small?
God will help you through them all
If you are suffering pain or grief
He will give you great relief

God is always at your side
And to Him you can confide
He will help to get you through
To find relief and comfort too

If your pain does not subside
With everything you have tried
Trust in God and praise Him too
He knows what is best for you

For everyone he has a plan
Let Him take you by the hand
God is your strength and refuge too
Always watching over you

Believe that when you seek Him out
He will come there is no doubt
When your trials are finally over
Eternal life will be yours forever
---fem

Poem inspired by Psalms chapters 23, 34 & 42

SHAME AND GUILT

What is guilt, what is shame?
Can you really give it a name?
So many feelings from way back
Some things that you have lacked

What people did to you is real
It makes you feel the way you feel
You try to go on with your life
As good as you can with all the strife

Forgive them, forgive yourself
Put bad feelings on a shelf
This is hard I know it is
But you'll feel better because of this

The feelings, the memories will always be there
They have to be dealt with using lots of care
It is important to take care of yourself too
No matter what was said or done to you

You are the number one in your life
On yourself you need to rely
Make yourself a better person
These have taught you many lessons

Change your thinking to the positive
You have a better life to live
Treat yourself with love and kindness
Be your real self and make your joys endless

---*fem*

SLEEP

I have all these thoughts when I go to bed
They're swimming all over inside my head
I want them to stop but they're always there
Sometimes I feel like pulling out my hair

I am so tired I want some sleep
Sometimes they make me want to weep
They just keep going around and around
No peace for me can be found

I can't stop thinking of so many things
so much tension that it brings
this makes me so stressed out
so stressed out that I want to shout

I cannot get these out of my head
I need some sleep, I need my bed
But awake I always stay
Later and later every day

I think of many things to do
Do they matter? Not even a few
It's just a reason for staying up late
The sleep I need just has to wait

I sit in a chair and fall asleep
This is a bad habit that I keep
I should listen to what I say
To go to bed but up I stay

Too tired to do a lot of things
Too tired to do anything
Everywhere I keep falling asleep
I need to get out of this hole so deep

I need to calm myself down at night
So I can sleep, it's such a fight
If this keeps up it will ruin my health
But I keep doing it in spite of myself

It's time to go to bed now
I need to get there somehow
I'm listening to myself tonight
I'm going to bed now, goodnight

---fem

SO DIM

The fog is creeping in
Everything seems so dim
Why are the days so dreary
Why do they make me weary

It's hard to stay on top of things
When this is what winter brings
It makes me feel all dull inside
Distracted and tired, I sigh

Not feeling like doing a thing
Such boredom and not caring
This keeps going day after day
There must be a better way

This is not what I want for me
I want some joy in life, you see
Full of cheer and a smile
That goes on for miles and miles

Winter is just one season
So what is the reason
My depression is here
And keeps going throughout the year

I have good days now and then
But it keeps coming back again
I just can't let it get me down
It's worth fighting all this, I've found

One good day is such a relief
To just forget about my grief
Is there something that I lack
As my depression keeps coming back

Is there a magic wand out there
If there is, please do share
These feelings aren't just my own
So many have them, but I feel so alone
---fem

SO DOWN TODAY

I feel so down today
I hope this goes away
So isolated and alone
The fight is all my own

I need to get my feelings up
I need for this all to stop
Why does this happen so often
My bad moods need to soften

I need to get out of here
To be with someone it is clear
But where do I go, what do I do
Please give me just one clue

Will it help to go to the store
Or will I need to do more
How many people should I see
With whom do I go who should it be

Is there someone out there
With whom I can really share
So I won't be so alone and blue
Please tell me, is it you?
---fem

SO EMOTIONAL

Sometimes I'm happy in my life
Sometimes I'm lonely not being your wife
My emotions have highs and lows
That's the way my life goes

Sometimes I am content just doing my own thing
Then something happens and my emotions swing
I cry so easily over things that I never used to
It seems to just happen which I don't want it to

Sometimes I feel so unstable I don't know what to do
Other times I can do whatever I want to
How do you keep all your feelings in control
When you feel like you are in a deep, deep hole

Sometimes I have anxiety or a panic attack
Then I turn around and good feelings are back
I dream of things I would like to do
But then I am afraid to do them too

So many different feelings racing in my head
And I get so sleepy but I don't go to bed
I seem to procrastinate way too much
And I would like to give myself a great big punch

But then again, I do enjoy doing crafts and things
And being with family, what a joy that brings
So many emotions coming from deep inside
Lots of them are things that I just want to hide

I just want to be who I was meant to be
To be free and able to be just me
To be able to feel normal and not so shy
And doing lots of things, not to just get by

I am so full of emotions today and need to let them out
I need to change myself there is no doubt
But I don't know how or where to start
I need a lot of help before I fall apart
---fem

SO MUCH TO BE DONE

So much to be done
But no motivation
You have things you can do
But nothing suits you

I could do this, I could do that
But none of it makes me react
Things I've been interested in before
Don't interest me anymore

I wander around wondering what to do
With all of these things staring at you
Nothing feels good, nothing seems right
Nothing is done when day turns to night

How can I get myself going again
To do things I enjoy and am interested in
Right now they bore me, they're no fun
I try but I can't find even one

Oh how empty my days feel
They pass me by and don't feel real
I feel like I am all burnt out
That's how I feel without a doubt

How can I get out of this rut
How can I get this all unstuck
What can I do to turn this around
So some joy can again be found

---fem

SO TIRED

I am so tired I don't know what to do
There are so many things I'm going through
I feel just so worn out
Too many things to think about

So much is spinning in my head
So much I can't even get to bed
What's the answer to all of this
A nice clear head is what I wish

The doctors say things that aren't clear
I don't know exactly what I hear
I want all of this to go away
To be better tomorrow than today

I have no energy to keep going
No motivation to keep on doing
So many things I don't care to do
My mind feels empty but yet so full

I need to get out of this place
To get my head back on pace
But I don't know how to get there
I need to be given the answer
---fem

SPRING

It looks like spring is finally here
This brings to me so much cheer
The trees are so very green
With lots of blossoms to be seen

My weeping willow survived the winter
It is growing faster than ever
This brings to me so much pleasure
It was planted with memories to treasure

A fresh new season has begun
To enjoy not just for me but everyone
I am determined this will be a start
For me to not fall all apart

I will try so very hard
To keep all the negative thoughts barred
Another chance to be so driven
To live the life that I've been given

Make this a new beginning
With a happy heart winning
Try to keep yourself up
And don't ever, ever stop
---*fem*

THE SUN

The sun is shining and it feels so good
Will tomorrow's rain change my mood?
We definitely need the rain though
So the crops will be able to grow

We need a mixture of weather
To make everything grow better
Snow, rain and sunshine
Are all needed in their time

The corn, the hay, the wheat too
If we were without, what would we do
All the animals that give meat
Are something else we can eat

All the vegetables in the garden grow
We need their nutrients that I know
It would be a problem so terrible
If these foods were not available

Although I love to see the sun
And be in the warmth having fun
The snow and the rain are needed too
To live without them would be so hard to do

My moods may change as does the weather
Sometimes worse, sometimes better
But when all is said and done
I really do like the sun!
---fem

TIRED

Three or four hours of sleep a night
For me this is quite a plight
Tired all day, falling asleep in a chair
I fall asleep no matter when or where

When night comes I sleep so fast
But my sleep just doesn't last
This keeps going on and on
I wish this problem would be gone

To stay awake I have a prescription
Hypersomnia is my condition
Why I don't sleep longer is a mystery
How much more tired can I be

I drive and go over the line
So glad nothing happened this time
What is causing this I wonder
Why can't I sleep a little longer

This problem needs a solution
An answer has to come to fruition
It would be nice if I could say
I am awake and alert each day

---fem

TOO GOOD TO BE TRUE

I knew it was too good to be true
To feel so good all day through
To have more days better than not
I knew that soon it would stop

Unexpected things came about
That made me sad without a doubt
Now I'm not so cheery again
Not like I was because of them

Why does this have to be
Why can't I enjoy being me
When good things happen to me
It soon turns around and attacks me

Always something to spoil how I feel
So afraid to be happy and real
Can't get too close to anyone
I will lose them and have no one

This has happened too many times
It seems being happy is a crime
Is it me? Is it them? What could it be
Why does this keep happening to me

Is this the way life is meant to be
Having happy spoiled by bad for me
Can you enjoy your life with all this
There is so much I don't want to miss

---fem

UNAWARE

People can be so unaware
And so many just don't care
In a bad mood is very hard
You need to be on your guard

Some people can be so toxic
Not friends you want to pick
Don't withdraw from who you are
You are more important by far

Choose to be better than that
For you know where you're at
Hear what issues others have
Empathize and share with them

Keep up the fight for you
Balance is what's good to do
You are worth so much more
There are better days in store
---fem

UP AND DOWN

My depression I have found
Is like a rollercoaster going up and down
Sometimes screaming, sometimes fun
And not knowing what will come

Then a twister comes to the ground
Everything I built turned upside down
To restore it is hard to do
But you know it will be good for you

Depression always seems to be lurking
Especially when what you try isn't working
It catches you quickly, in a snap
And it makes you feel like crap

When the good times come around
Treasure the good that you have found
Seek a way to get you through
The next time all this happens to you

It is hard, not easy to do
But the strength is inside of you
Be determined and strike back
Be ready for the next attack
---fem

VISITING MY DAUGHTER

I'm visiting my daughter today
How wonderful it is to stay
It is so peaceful here
I am so full of cheer

The grass, the trees
So many shades of green
What a beautiful scene
I feel so serene

No problems am I facing
My mind has not been racing
It is good to feel this way
And it happens every day

It is so good to relax
I know I will be coming back
This has been a good trip you see
Clearing my head is good for me
---*fem*

WHAT'S GOING ON

I just don't know what's going on
My concentration seems to be gone
I can't keep doing what I start
It feels like I am falling apart

What is so wrong with me
What oh what can it be
I feel like I am in a fog
That I am a bump on a log

So much distraction is a bother
I go from one thing to another
Never satisfied with what I'm doing
Why can't I get myself going

Important bills I missed paying
What is all of this saying
I need to get this out of my head
Feeling like this is what I dread

I need to shape up and shake it off
I have really had enough
I am so tired of all of this
Feeling good is what I miss

---*fem*

WHERE DO I GO?

Where do I go from here
My thoughts are not very clear
I cannot seem to think at all
Just curl myself into a ball

The feeling is not pleasant
I just can't stay in the present
My mind is all over the place
Seems each thought is having a race

I just want to make it stop
Before my head begins to pop
I'm getting so very tired of this
There's so much in life I don't want to miss

Can today be a brand-new start
Or will I again be falling apart
How can I get things under control
Will I ever reach my goal

I know it would be good for me
To have places to go and people to see
Right now I feel so very down
I don't want anyone around

Am I just feeling sorry for myself
Or is it really my mental health
I want to change in either case
I want my mind in a better place

So many reasons I want to live
So much of myself I'd like to give
I need to get started somehow
No time to waste, it has to be now
---fem

WHY

Why does it happen
Why is it so often
You can feel so good, you're on top of the world
The next moment into a ball you are curled

Why can you be happy hearing the birds sing
Then in a wink you don't like anything
All of this makes me perplexed
Why when you're happy depression comes next

It's like the weather when it's warm and sunny
And then it's raining and nothing is funny
Why is it when you're enjoying it all
The next minute you're not speaking at all

So happy to be with people you know
And then cry because you're all alone
Why does this happen so many times
Why does my head keep changing its mind

Something has to be done about this
So many things that I miss
But what can I do, where can I go
This is something I don't know

Can you tell me why this happens to me
I'm tired of not being able to see
How can I change all of this somehow
I want the answer and I want it now.

---fem

WHY CAN'T I CRY?

Since I was young I couldn't cry
Though I was sad I could only sigh
Being laughed at and told to be tough
Being called a "cry baby" was really rough

I learned not to show my true feelings
To hide them all and concealing
Though many years have gone by
I still find it hard to cry

Ashamed if I cry for someone to see
I try to hold it inside of me
If I cry when I'm alone
I try to stop not let it all go

Why is it that even now
My childhood comes back somehow
So many things I learned back then
Keep coming back again and again

People tell me it's okay
But these thoughts won't go away
I still feel the things that were
In my mind so many years

If I start crying I need to stop
All my old feelings still showing up
How can I start letting them out
To cry, get angry and to shout

---fem

WHY DO I CRY?

I really don't know why
I feel like I'm going to cry
Is there something wrong with me
Something that I do not see

So emotional do I get
I have not figured it out yet
I seem to cry at the drop of hat
But I try to hide all that

So overwhelmed do I feel
Tell me, are my feelings real
So distracted do I get
I have no concentration yet

So many things don't get done
Not just a few, not just one
My mind keeps wandering everywhere
Where in the world do I go from here

I want to relax and enjoy my time
So good feelings can be mine
I want my life to have some space
And put my emotions in their place

Is there any peace for me
In the future can you see
What can I do to change all this
I have a life I don't want to miss

---fem

WHY IS IT?

Why is it when you're feeling good
Just like you think you should
Depression keeps on coming back
What is it that I lack?

I know there is something wrong
I no more hum any songs
I'm going to that dark, dark place
No longer a smile upon my face

In its place is a big frown
It's like I'm falling to the ground
Can I get up again
If I do, will I feel better then?

I need to get out of this place
Things in my head are starting to race
Distractions are everywhere
My concentration is not there

Sleep is something that I lack
I need to fight to keep on track
Need to keep this from returning again
Will I be better, if so, when?

---fem

WITH YOU

Grief should not be treated lightly
It keeps on no matter how you try
They say feeling better will take time
But it seems forever will not make me fine

Then there is depression too
It's always there inside of you
Sometimes you have days you feel bad
This will make you tired and sad

But then it turns around for you
And you feel like doing things too
These are all trying times
You need to try to get by

Take a step forward one at a time
You may step back but please try
To take another forward step
So feeling better can be kept

Don't stop fighting and trying too
We want things to get better for you
And no matter what you do
We are always here for you
---fem

MY DAUGHTER'S POEMS

I have been blessed with a family of many diverse talents. My daughter, Bobbi, has been writing contemporary Christian songs and putting them on YouTube™. Some of the lyrics are actually poems. I asked if I could include a couple of them in my book as the words bring out so many emotions. After reading them, I am sure you will agree.

Illustrated by Lizzie Ostermann

THAT DAY ON THE PLAYGROUND
By Bobbi Ostermann

That day on the playground,
Engrained in my mind
The girls in my class
Were anything but kind

"You are ugly," they said
"And you are so fat"
"Nobody likes you,
You're worthless, take that!"

They spent the whole recess
With their verbal attack
As I just sat quietly,
Afraid to fight back

I did not react,
They didn't see me cry
I remained stoic
Though tears stung my eyes

My mind drifted away,
I made a diversion in my head
To protect my heart
From the words being said

Recess was over,
So I got up to walk
Silently across the playground
I did not talk

No one to tell,
I wouldn't dare
I kept my mouth shut
Because who'd even care.

THREAD OF HOPE
By Bobbi Ostermann

When my life is overwhelming
When the darkness tries to drown me
And I can't seem to find my way

When anxiety is rising
And my worry tries to hold me down
Barely strength for one more day

My sanity is waning
The walls are closing in
I'm running out of strength to carry on

I'm searching for a Thread of Hope

When I'm feeling like a failure
And afraid I've let too many down
And I'm too ashamed to ask for help

When I'm sitting all alone, here
And afraid no one will understand
Or that no one would even care

When I'm chained by condemnation
Bound by chains that I have made myself
I need someone to set me free

I'm searching for a Thread of Hope

Lord, You're My Hope
My Thread of Hope
Come set me free
Free me of me

I've built these walls around my heart
Afraid that I might be found out
I don't want anyone to see

All my imperfections
All the storms that rage inside of me
I know that they'll abandon me

But I have to let somebody in
I cannot go on this way
I'm searching for a Thread of Hope

Lord, You're My Hope
My Thread of Hope
Come set me free
Free me of me

Lord, break these chains
Smash these walls
Help me, Lord
Make them fall

I'm reaching for my Thread of Hope

Pull me up into Your grace
Hold me in Your warm embrace
Hem me in Your Thread of Hope

Lord, you are My Thread of Hope

GRIEF

Grief also requires getting your feelings out as mentioned above with depression. If you have both it's really tough to go on without letting someone know how you feel. I write poems for this. Journaling, making lists, etc. are helpful in the challenge and changes you are going through. My husband passed away three years ago, but so many days it feels like it just happened. There are so many emotions going through you. There is sadness of your loss, your missing him, being overwhelmed as you need to take over everything and trying to move forward to make your life better. Like I said before, it is a very tough thing to get through, but I am determined to succeed.

Illustrated by Addie Slominsky

I came upon this the other day. I don't even remember which one of our children wrote this. They all thought so much of their dad.

Dear God, I gratefully thank you for giving me my Dad.
You must really love me,
'cause you gave the best you had.

We will miss the sound of your voice and the way you tell your stories, jokes, and even snore.

We will miss the Sunday drives, watching Packer games and talks about the farm.

We will miss finding you reading at the kitchen table or napping on your chair.

Thank you for leading by example and showing us how to love, and teaching and preparing us for the hard lessons of life and death.

77 years was not enough for us, but it was a lifetime for you.

Now, go and celebrate the most glorious birthday of them all.

Happy 1st Heavenly Birthday!

DECORATING THE TREE

As I decorate the tree this year
I can't help shed a few tears
Every ornament that I put there
Is a memory of a time we shared

I feel like he is here with me
But I don't see him, can it be?
I hung the barn with the farmer and wife
And his tractor that shows his life

One for Grandpa and Grandma is there
Telling us of their love and why they cared
Others just bring back many memories to me
Of a time in the past that will never again be

Though they make me sad now
They make me feel good some how
They are ornaments I'll cherish always
And he'll be with me every Christmas Day
---fem

NEW YEARS DAY

Christmas day has come and gone
We opened presents one by one
Some made us happy some sad
But all in all it wasn't that bad

New Years Day is coming on
Will you be celebrating this one
It's a time for a brand-new start
A time to share what's in your heart

A new year full of laughter and love
Doing things you've been dreaming of
Though you may also shed some tears
For those you've loved throughout the years

We'll hope this year is a better one
Hoping better times will come
So enjoy the new year coming to you
I wish this for all of you
---fem

GONE SO LONG

You've been gone for just so long
And I have tried to remain strong
Yet I expect you when I turn around
But you are nowhere to be found

Sometimes I can feel you with me
But I'm the only one I see
You always seem to be so near
But there's no voice for me to hear

Are you here, can it be
Or is my mind playing tricks on me
I remember all the little things
Each new day would always bring

I miss your giving me advice
And at times you'd tell me twice
So much I would depend on you for
The things that I would always ignore

All the feelings we had for each other
Are just memories from one time or another
The time has gone just too quickly
I wish you were still standing with me

But I know this cannot be
Things in life happen, you see
I'll be okay and keep going on
For you'll be with me all along

---fem

STRUGGLE

What a struggle these two years have been
It seems like today not back then
I remember every moment of that day
The day my love was taken away

The kids have grown so much since then
He would be so very proud of them
Time is going so very fast
But I want his memory to last

All of his things are in the same place
As if he was still here and I can see his face
I don't want to lose any thoughts of him
Though I know eventually some will grow dim

I am trying to move forward
But it is so hard
Sometimes I don't know what to do
How do I keep going when I miss you

He wouldn't want me to be sad
He'd want my life to go on and be glad
Though everything seems so grim
I need to try to honor him

---fem

FORGIVE ME

I feel so bad about things I thought
When you were here what I forgot
All the things that you did
No appreciation did you win

There was so much you couldn't do
I thought I was doing everything too
But now I find how much you did
I don't know what to replace it with

I'm getting along that I know
But it's so hard, you helped me so
No compensation for what you did for me,
Doing things I did not see

I realize now what you did for me
I always depended on you, you see
The little chores that you could do
I do them but they remind me of you

You kept me on track to do things on time
That was a big lack of mine
You always advised me on what to do
And also when the bills were due

It seems I will never keep up
Doing all the things it never stops
You always helped through the difficult times
And your memory was good not like mine

I'm sorry I didn't appreciate you more
Because you were the one I adored
I'm sorry I got irritated with you
Please forgive me for I love you
---fem

"Repent, then and turn to God, so that your sins may be wiped out, that times of refreshing may come from the Lord." Acts 3:19

MIXED FEELINGS

My mind is just so mixed up
Sometimes I cry and can't stop
But then I go on with my life
Not thinking of him which doesn't feel right

Someone says or brings up something
And oh the sadness that it brings
Then I have a good time with someone
But I still miss him because he's gone

How can your mind keep turning around
It feels like it's going around and around
I think of him then I cry
When I don't I feel guilty, why?

There's so much of him here
So many memories I hold dear
But then my life goes on
Not thinking of him, is that wrong?

He's not here and I miss him so much
I know he's someone I can't touch
I need to go on with just me
But the future I cannot see

I know he'd want me to be happy too
But I just don't know what to do
I try but it's so hard for me
To feel good without him you see

What can I do, where can I go
These are things I'd like to know
To enjoy my life as it is
When I feel so much like this

---fem

MEMORIES

The memories keep coming back to me
And wondering how can it be
It seems that he's still here in some way
I feel he's just gone for the day

The memories seem so very real
Oh how sad they make me feel
Remembering him lying in his bed
The songs and prayers that were said

Holding his hand at his bedside
Watching him slowly die
I remember his last gurgling breath
As he was taken into death

All the family was near
But their words I could not hear
I lost my only love that day
I've been so sad since he went away

Though over two years have gone by
These memories still make me cry
I try to go on alone
But this is such an empty home

I can't stop thinking of him
And some days seem so very grim
But there are days that are not so bad
Remembering all the good times we had

With my life I need to keep going
This is something I need knowing
But it is so hard to do
When I am missing so much of you

---fem

FUNERAL

Death has come to me again
A reminder of who I lost and when
I'm afraid to go to the funeral
Will I cry more than a little?

I don't want them to see me cry
How in the world will I get by
This death makes me so sad
Is my crying really bad?

I have so much trouble with this
There are so many things I miss
Because I am afraid to cry
No matter when, no matter why

Will they think less of me
Because my feelings they will see
I just can't let my feelings show
I just can't let them really know

I need to have courage for this
To let it go and dismiss
Disregard all of their thoughts
When they see me cry a lot

Will this happen? I don't know
I wish I could let my feelings go
But I'm so afraid they'll come out
So afraid they'll see me, no doubt

This feels so important to me
That my feelings they don't see
But I want to change it so
To let myself cry, to let go

This is one of my struggles now
That I need to let go somehow
I just don't know how to change it
Can you help me and explain it?
---fem

GRIEF

My grief is still here it is not gone
Why does it keep hanging on
It hurts to still think of him
To remember his laughter again

It hurts to be so lonely
To not see his face before me
I feel like a big branch in the river
With the water swirling all over

The current is so very strong
But the branch doesn't flow along
It's stuck in the swirl going round and round
Will it ever get loose and float down

This grief is so complicated
With many feelings conglomerated
Not just one but many intertwined
Into the grief that is in my mind

No matter how much I shout and shout
The grief won't leave, it won't go out
I am stuck in this sad place
Wishing this time could be erased

---*fem*

MISSING HIM

I really miss him, I truly do
But I want to make a life for me too
My mind is so very mixed up
I don't want his memory to stop

But I don't like being this way
Stuck in the past all day
How can I keep his memory alive
If I leave it, how will I survive

I don't want to forget him
Or lose touch with the past
The feelings we had then
How long will they last

I need to keep going on so bad
But I don't want to lose what we had
I know it will never be the same
He'll never be there when I speak his name

It's been quite a while since he died
But I am still so lonely inside
I hold onto his things to keep him close
That is how my life goes

Never forgetting all that I lack
Knowing his presence will never come back
I need to go on, that is for sure
But how in the world can I endure

A life without him is hard to face
Feeling like I'm losing a race
So many feelings inside of me
The future is too blurry to see

He wouldn't want me to be this way
He'd want me to be happy every day
How can I live up to this
When so much of him I really miss
              ---*fem*

AWOKE

I woke up as I do every day
Feeling tired, I am that way
But when I turned just a little
I felt him there in the middle

What is the deal
I know it's not real
Why does this keep happening to me
Feeling he's there but I can't see

So many times, this has happened
It makes me feel so bad, so saddened
Why can't this all go away
And just have all his memories stay

So many times I feel him with me
Is it so? How can it be
Very close his presence seems
What does all of this mean

Should I feel happy he is there
Is it real? This isn't fair
It makes me think of his death
I remember his very last breath

How can I get any peace
When all this just doesn't cease
How can I move forward like this
Feeling him there but his presence I miss

These things just keep popping up
Why can't they go away and stop
How do I keep going on
When my true love has gone

God please help me every day
Keep me from feeling this way
Please stay with me, help me cope
I can't do it alone, please give me hope
---fem

MISS YOU MORE

Christmas is coming and I miss you more
So much more than I ever did before
I'm having a rough time without you
And I just don't know what to do

Friends and family are around
So a little happiness can be found
But when I am alone
I think of you and want you home

You were my rock and now it's crumbled
Right now it seems my troubles have doubled
I don't know what the future holds
I'm afraid and it seems so cold

I need you to put me at ease
Especially now with this disease
I don't know how to keep going
To handle all of this unknowing

I try to keep going day by day
But it doesn't seem to be working that way
I try not to think too much
It's hard, I need to lean on your crutch

Today has been a really hard one
I'm trying but I can't get things done
Your memories are lurking
Nothing seems to be working

I need just a little thread of hope
I need it to help me cope
I am in despair
I need that thread to make repairs
---fem

TOO MUCH

So much is going around in my mind
Things to do that were falling behind
My grief has been so overwhelming
Not being alert or understanding

Now everything is coming at me
Things that before I just couldn't see
Doctors, lawyers, bankers and such
So worried I feel, can't eat my lunch

My head still whirling when I go to bed
All these things to do that I dread
I lie there awake, can't get to sleep
An everyday occurrence that I keep

So many things I have been told
Is this what happens when you get old?
You just don't know what will happen next
It all makes me feel so very perplexed

One tells you this the other that
Walking all over me like I'm a mat
Each one says they're right not wrong
Decisions for me are taking so long

So much coming at me I can't think straight
That is something I really hate
What do I do, where do I go
About these things I just don't know

Things were so good when he was here
He would make everything so clear
But now I'm doing it on my own
Oh how I hate being alone
---fem

"Even in laughter the heart may ache, and rejoicing may end in grief"
Proverbs 14:13

CHRISTMASTIME IS HERE

Christmastime is here
Christmas Day is drawing near
Full of love, laughter and fun
But I'll be missing someone

As we enjoy the holiday
With family and friends that day
You will not be near
But in our thoughts so dear

The same Christmas will never be
It changed when you left you see
We'll still be happy and enjoy it too
But it will be different without you
---fem

TIME

The days just go flying by
They don't slow down though I try
So many changes I can't keep up
Sometimes I wish it all would stop

Reality turns into memories so quick
It's hard to remember, it just doesn't stick
I want those good times to come back
To feel the joy that I now lack

I miss so much, the past is gone
Now alone I travel on
To go on is so hard to do
Knowing how much I'm missing you

Sometimes you seem so real to me
But when I look I do not see
Sometimes I can feel you near
But that brings to me more tears

Nothing will ever be the same
Not even when I call out your name
You won't be there when I say
I love you more and more each day

I can't go back to change a thing
But I can't help remembering
All the times good and bad
How happy we were, but now I'm sad

All I have are memories
All the past is what I see
Moving forward I need to go
But how to do it I don't know
---fem

THE OTHER NIGHT

I was at a place the other night
Where I just didn't feel quite right
A place where you used to host
Where you would tell so many jokes

So many people were there having fun
But I felt I was missing someone
Thoughts of you kept coming to me
I was alone with a crowd all around me

It's been a few years, almost three
But my grief keeps going on endlessly
It seems as though time has stood still
With a void in my life I cannot fill

I am brought back so many times
to your last breath with your hand in mine
wanting you to be with me always
but wanting your struggle to go away

Though leaving me would be best for you
I couldn't help being selfish too
These feelings were so conflicting
And my heart was slowly breaking

I let you go to be with God
Without pain, you'd have His love
Knowing there will be a time when
I will be seeing you again

---*fem*

CARRY ON

I have no hope to carry on
No wish to live like this - alone
I lost my only love today
How can I even find my way

It seems like I have lost everything
Oh how his death does sting
It seems my life has no purpose now
I need to go on but I don't know how

I hear the words of sympathy
But they mean nothing to me
The hugs, the tears, the kind gestures
Are something I just can't endure

How will I be able to live like this
When the sight of you I miss
I don't know how I can stay
When you are so very far away

Then I hear a voice like yours
Telling me not to close my door
Keep it open to let people in
They will help you be happy again

It will take a while to see
And you will have all my memories
Don't worry at all about me
This is a glorious place to be

I have hope you can do this
This for you is what I wish
May you have the hope to go on
I'll be there when your journey is done
---fem

DO YOU STILL LOVE ME?

Do you still love me from up there
Do you think of me, do you care
Are you one of those twinkling stars
Oh so far away you are

I thought by now my sadness would soften
But I cry for you so often
I miss every part of you
But there is nothing I can do

I know you're happy where you are
But I can't see you, you're too far
I hope you can see the things I do
I hope that you are proud of me too

I have missed you every day
Since the day you went away
You've been gone for so long
But my emptiness feels so very strong

If you are watching from above
Know my heart is full of our love
A love like ours will always be
Now and in eternity

---fem

MISS YOU TODAY

I am missing you today
So much more than yesterday
I can't get used to not having you here
So much to tell that you can't hear

The rooms are so silent now
I need to fill the void somehow
I am feeling so all alone
It feels like such an empty home

I can't depend on you anymore
That makes me miss you so much more
All by myself there's so much to do
that we did together, just us two

So many things we used to share
The times you told me that you care
I don't hear those things anymore
My tears are dripping to the floor

Oh how sad I am today
How can I make it all go away
How long will it take to fill this hole
How long will it take for me to feel whole
---fem

A NEW JOURNEY

I have begun a new journey. These poems are my feelings after being newly diagnosed with Parkinsonism. It is something I never expected and am learning to deal with it. As a degenerative condition with no cure, it is very scary not knowing how much it will progress or how fast. I am trying to live one day at a time and live that day to the fullest. The rest is up to God. I trust in Him knowing what is right for me and that He will be with me all the way.

WHAT TO DO

God, I don't know what to do
I need to put my trust in You
I don't know if I can handle this
So many things I don't want to miss

What's in the future I cannot tell
Will it progress or will I feel well
I'm healthy in so many ways
How long will it take, how many days

I need Your help to get me through
I need to be able to count on You
The future ahead is so scary
The results of this can be so varied

I know some people in this condition
I don't want to be in that situation
But it is all in Your hands
You know the things You have planned

Is there hope that this isn't true
that it will get better for me too
I just don't know what to think
My happiness is starting to sink

Give me strength and help me see
The path that lies ahead for me
Be with me through each day
Take care of me in every way

Comfort, love and peace I need
To go on with this indeed
Don't ever, ever leave my side
And with me, please abide
----fem

"Peace, I leave with you; my peace I give you. I do not give to you as the world gives. Do not let your hearts be troubled and do not be afraid."
John 14:26 NIV

DEPRESSED

You hear the bad news
Something you wouldn't choose
You get depressed
You know the rest

The days are dreary
You get weary
The thoughts keep going in your head
Do you remember what he said?

How do you stop feeling down
This attitude needs to turn around
Staying this way is not good
You feel worse than you really should

Turning all of this around
Is what I want to be found
It is so hard to change your thoughts
To use the skills you've been taught

They always say baby steps to take
To celebrate the progress you make
But sometimes I don't feel this way
And then here comes another day

A day full of darkness and sadness
Words I cannot even express
Can I ever be happy again
If I can, tell me when

Try and try the thoughts keep coming
I really need to do something
I can't keep going on this way
Day after day after day

Listening to the thoughts I have
Is not good but very bad
More energy I also need
Please let it come with great speed

I need to feel like myself again
I just don't know how or when
Help for this is what I need
Help to plant that first seed

To grow into who I want to be
Is something right now I cannot see
Feeling better I need to get
Not knowing when it will happen yet

---fem

DEPRESSION IN THE BIBLE

God has a plan for each one
He gives us hope when we have none
Try to persevere and pray
Every night and every day

Give to Him all your cares
Don't give in to your despair
Follow God's directions fully
Don't let depression be your bully

Though you may have many sorrows
Look to God for your tomorrows
If you're feeling scorned and alone
Remember Jesus calls you His own

Do not doubt, have reassurance
The Word of God is your insurance
Keep the Devil's temptations at bay
Don't give in, he likes it that way

Get bad news or facing death
And you feel you have nothing left
The Word will surely comfort you
God, our Lord will see you through

Even though your depression feels bad
Look at the sorrow and grief Jesus had
If you do wrong and think no one cares
Repent and seek forgiveness in prayer

You may have doubt from your depression
Know that Jesus is your salvation
Turn to God and don't give in
Have hope in the Lord and you will win
---fem

DISCUSSION

It was discussed today
Is there a situation in some way
Someone would welcome death
Rather than live their given path

This brought many things to mind
I'm in a situation of this kind
Looking at Parkinson progression
Having a lifelong depression

I don't think they realized
There were tears in my eyes
This was not of my choosing
Thinking of things I would be losing

But I need to realize this fact
I can't control how life will act
It's all in God's hands, you see
He knows what is best for me

What will the future bring
He knows everything
All I can do right now
Is to do my best somehow

Keep believing and trusting Him
Though right now it feels so grim
I need to have Him take my hand
As He leads me on the path He planned

He will always be at my side
Through my journey He will guide
He will comfort and take care of me
His love is there, I know that to be

My faith is stronger, that I know
And He will never let me go
I know when life ends for me
I'll be living with Him eternally
---fem

TOO ANXIOUS

I'm on yet another journey
One I wouldn't have planned for me
A diagnosis so unexpected
But symptoms that I presented

There is no cure
Of that it's clear
But where do I go from here
What will happen in the coming years

My anxiety is getting very high
On my mind no matter what I try
How do I cope
Is there hope

What will happen to me
The days ahead I cannot see
I try to fight it so it won't progress
But I get so tired and distressed

I can't let it get a hold on me
Can't give up or just let it be
I don't want to be its pawn
So I need to keep very calm

I have to keep a positive attitude
And stay in a positive mood
Need to keep on with exercises
But my anxiety still rises

Would it help to talk to someone
Would that make my anxiety gone
I need an answer to that question
How can I make that connection

What will happen and how fast
How long will my movements last
Will I be able to stay alone
will I be able to stay in my home

So many things to think about
All in my head - I want to shout
This is not good for me
It raises my anxiety

My stomach is upset
I can't sleep or think straight
It is always on my mind
But peace I cannot find

So afraid what will happen next
I am so very perplexed
My depression is getting worse
Feels like my head will burst

Help for this needs to be found
Is there anything around
Is there anything I can do
To keep all this from coming true

Lord please help me to get through
I need to trust in You
Give me strength and comfort too
Send Your love and tell me what to do

Please give me the peace I need
All of this is my plea
Keep my faith strong
No matter what goes wrong

Guide my path as I go
Into a future I don't know
Be with me every day
As I go along my way

I give You all my problems now
I know You will fix them somehow
Praise to the father and to the Son
And to the Holy Spirit Three in One
---fem

"...In Me you may have peace. In this world you will have trouble. But take heart! I have overcome the world."
John 16:33

PATIENCE

Make me patient, keep me calm
Four months have already gone
No improvement has been seen
What does that really mean?

He upped my dose hoping to find
A more definitive diagnosis of some kind
It just takes time to get results
It's not really anyone's fault

To figure it out just takes so long
I just want to know what is wrong
So many unanswered questions
Things that I forgot to mention

Four more months waiting to find out
Then will I know exactly what it's about
Hoping things don't get worse until then
As I wait wondering again and again

I don't want the time to go fast
I just want to get answers at last
So keep me patient, keep me calm
Until we find out what exactly is wrong
---fem

THINKING

Don't think, don't think, I cannot think
If I do my mood will sink
It takes me where I don't want to go
To a place that I would rather not know

Sometimes thinking makes me sad
Other times I just feel bad
Thinking also makes me scared
Things like this I cannot share

It especially hurts when I am grieving
Thinking of people who are leaving
It makes me wonder about my PD
How in the future it will affect me

Thinking makes me feel all alone
Making me anxious of things unknown
All this thinking makes me cry
And it makes me wonder why

Thinking comes so easy for me
Thinking of things I don't want to see
I try to avoid it but it always comes back
Sometimes I think I will crack

How can I stop all the negative things
The thoughts and feelings that it brings
I try to stay busy doing things I like
but it comes back like a lightning strike

Is there an answer to this dilemma I face
Or is it something I cannot erase
This thinking is really getting to me
I want it to end, for my mind to be free
---fem

WAITING

I'm waiting in anticipation today
Wondering what the doctor will say
Will it be good or will it be bad
Will it make me happy or sad

Will I be able to handle it
Or fall apart a little bit
Will it be what I'm afraid of
Will it progress, will it be rough

So many questions to ask him
But will the answers be grim
Maybe it won't be so bad
But I'm afraid of what I have

I shouldn't worry or think so much
It only makes things more tough
I've been trying to do what they say
To keep myself going in a good way

But my sleeping has not improved
Sometimes my balance is off when I move
I'm trying to fight it as best I can
I'm too stubborn to ask for a hand

Yes, I'm wondering what he will say
At my appointment on Monday
I need to keep calm until then
To be prepared when I see him again
---fem

MISCELLANEOUS

The following are poems of some of my daily life experiences. Many of them show my faith in God which is very important to me. They are my personal beliefs and not intended to offend anyone. Some of the poems may not be completely understandable as they have a personal meaning behind them. I do hope, however, that you enjoy them.

Illustrated by Karlie Marks

A LOVING PRAYER

This brings to you a loving prayer
That God will keep you in His care
You have a great loss today
No one can take the pain away

It will be a tough road to follow
And you will have so much sorrow
You will hear what people say
They mean good but it hurts anyway

But through it all you will be
A stronger person, wait and see
From all the love you've had for years
Each little memory you will hold dear

God will give you grace and peace
God's love for you will never cease
He has a plan we do not know
But we must trust Him as we go

May God's loving arms hold you close
Giving the peace you need the most
May he help you find your way
As He takes you through each day
---fem

WHEN WORDS FALL SHORT

There are no words to say
for the sadness you have today
Just thoughts and prayers for you
That God will take care of you

May He give you peace and strength
May He be your comfort at length
May He hold you in His arms with love
And watch over you from above
---fem

UNCONDITIONAL

As you grieve your loss today
My thoughts and prayers are on the way
May God give you strength and peace
Give you comfort that will not cease

May he keep you in his care
This for you is my prayer
Feel His loving arms holding you
He will help to see you through
---fem

GRAND DAUGHTER'S POEM

My granddaughter, Erin, wrote this poem for me as a Christmas gift. You probably won't understand all that she talks about, but it is something I will always cherish.

To Grandma:

You are a great poet
And we all know it

So I thought I'd try it out
And give you a shoutout

You have a pretty smile
Even without a nose
You've got nice style
I love buying you clothes

Thank you for your unconditional love
It goes beyond and above

**Merry Christmas!
Love, Erin**

PEOPLE

These are poems about people who have touched my life in different ways. I have known some of them for a long time and others more recently. One is about a stranger who I may never see again.

TO JEFF

Thank you for all you have done
Because of you this was all begun
I am so glad I have gotten to know you
And I am proud of all you do

You've been supportive from the start
To the finishing of "Poems from the Heart"
Wishing you the best in all your endeavors
Hope we can keep in touch with each other
---fem

LOIS

Thank you for the caring person you are
You have helped me come so far
You were so very friendly
When I thought I didn't have any

You have helped me through so much
And within my heart you've touched
As you care for everyone
I'm glad for what you have done

Your light shines through
In all you do
Calling you my friend is what I do
I hope this is also true for you

Praise God for people like you
An example so very true
Of all the faith you have in Him
And the kindness you have given
---fem

LORRAINE

My sister is sick and doesn't look good
She can't do much, I wish she could
Her heart is bad, her body weak
Her speech is slow when she tries to speak

We've had so much fun having lunch together
It's been so good to know her better
Though our ages are quite far apart
She now has a bigger place in my heart

I don't know what will happen with her
Will she get better or worse, I'm not sure
But right now it doesn't look good
She just doesn't look like she should

I put this all in God's hands
Only He knows what's been planned
I pray if she goes it will be in peace
If she stays give her the patience she needs

Please Dear Lord take care of her
No matter what your answer
Keep her away from any harm
And hold her in Your loving arms

---fem

PASTOR APPRECIATION

You are both appreciated so very much
So many hearts you have touched
You have helped all of us so patiently
You have also been so good to me

The Word of God that you preach
Many souls it does reach
Your sermons are easy to understand
They feel like God is taking my hand

You are there for all our needs
You are there to help us grieve
You are there for the happy times too
That is why we appreciate you

There are so many things you do
To help us all, to see us through
These are only just a few
Of the many things that you do

If I would write all we like about you two
This wouldn't be a page but a book about you
So may God bless you in all you do
May He always be with you too

May He give you the strength to keep going
His help will come, He is all knowing
May God be with you every day
And answer your prayers in His own way

May God's light shine upon you
And be gracious to you too
As His light shines through you
To all of us too

We praise God, for we have been blessed
With two pastors who are the best
Thank you so very, very much
Our lives will be forever touched

---fem

RED

Red was one of the best
Now he has been put to rest
He will be missed by you and all
He's in a place where he's having a ball

A beautiful place is where he will be
Happier than we could ever think to be
But this doesn't make it any easier for you
And sometimes you won't know what to do

The sympathy cards, the words people say
May bring you comfort in their own way
If there is anything I can do
I'll do my best to help you through

God has a plan for all of us
It is in Him we can trust
He has helped us in so many ways
For our salvation give Him praise

Never give up on the Lord above
He is full of so much love
He will help you in every way
He'll be beside you every day
---fem

RUTH AND MARSHALL

HAPPY 50TH ANNIVERSARY to the two of you!
Your love shines through in everything you do
Keep on going for many years
Hold on to the memories they're so dear

You have had many hardships I know
You're always bright and thoughtful though
I'm so glad I met you two
I think so very much of you

Three children through the years you've raised
And thanked the Lord and gave him praise
They have grown into their own things
And God is with them, sing praise

Then there are your grandchildren
I can see the love every time you're with them
You have given them a model to go by
You show them God's love with a twinkle in your eye

So on this very happy day
I wish you God's blessings in every way
It is on Him you can depend
You know that Jesus is your friend

May He see you through good and bad
Cast on Him any cares you have
May He comfort you in times you're sad
And rejoice with you when you're glad

May He take care of your every need
Keep you safe from harm indeed
May He be with you always
Through your nights and through your days

May He shed His light upon you
May He be gracious to you
For His love will never cease
May He give you any needed peace
---fem

TERRI

I met this lady on the plane
At first, I didn't know her name
Waiting for our connection we talked
Neither of us could barely walk

Our families were our main topic
We just seemed to really click
As we waited for our next plane
We exchanged each other's names

What a great way to spend our time
She was so very kind
Although I may never see her again
I hope I can still call her my friend
---*fem*

VARIOUS THOUGHTS

Life has so many things to think about. These are some of the miscellaneous thoughts and feelings that I had with no particular category.

Illustrated by Lizzie Ostermann

ADDICTION

This chronic pain is getting to me
Things others cannot see
Try so many things to get better
Following directions to the letter

I felt so good yesterday
I wish I could always feel this way
The cause of this was my sedation
How easy it would be to have addiction

As it wore off I wanted more
So I would feel as I did before
But I know that just can't be
It would only mean trouble for me

I understand a little more
What I didn't know before
How easy it is to become addicted
It cannot be predicted

It could start with just one time
But develop into more to unwind
And so the cycle goes and goes
And where it stops no one knows

This snowballing effect is not good
Stay away from it as you should
Though how tempting it can be
to take one more to feel more free

Getting off is so hard to do
It has withdrawal symptoms too
Stay away from it from the start
If you don't you may fall apart
---fem

JOURNEY

We're on a journey in our life
Full of lots of sadness and strife
But God has blessed us all too
Giving family and friends to love you

This is a great journey on this earth
We can celebrate Jesus' holy birth
And until our earthly life ends
It is on God whom we can depend

Keep up the faith, it will keep you going
The Lord our God is all knowing
He will always take care of you
No matter what you say or do

He knows every moment to come
He knows when we'll reach His kingdom
But until then, while on earth we are here
We'll enjoy his creations and remember He's near

No matter how big or how small
Pray, He will listen to them all
You are in His great loving hands
Even after this earthly life ends
---fem

THE SEASONS

The sun beats down upon us
This weather seems so glorious
I love the flowers, the birds that sing
And everything that is Spring

It's a little warmer in the summer
Sometimes too hot 'til the sun goes under
Full of activities, ball games and such
Full of fun, I love it so much

Then all of a sudden fall is here
Which means that winter is getting near
The colorful trees are so very pretty
To see the leaves fall is such a pity

Before you know it, it is winter
Preparing the world for a brand-new year
The wind blows cold and snow falls
With a fire inside making it cozy for all

All of these seasons are their own
Each one comes and each one goes
They all have a purpose when they come
And make the world ready for the next one

How wonderful it is to see all of this
To be able to enjoy and not miss
The wonders that each one brings
A sight to behold, a reason to sing

When you get down and feel sad
Remember all the good times you had
Enjoying each season as it came
And knowing they will come again
---fem

TIME

Time just keeps on flying by
When did I get old? I wonder why
Today is going so very fast
Soon it will be a day in the past

Tomorrow will come and quickly go
How to stop it I just don't know
All of a sudden I am old
Onto my youth I want to hold

My back hurts, my body is stiff
I don't go as fast as I did
My concentration is getting bad
I get distracted which makes me sad

Doing one chore seems twice as long
I can't always fix the things that go wrong
I can't reach as high as I used to
Or do all the things I want to do

It's hard to accept help from others
Before you were the one helping another
Yes, getting old is no fun
But at least I'm not the only one

---fem

MY HOPE

Hope you have when things go wrong
And at times will make you strong
It is a faith that better will come
A faith we all share not just some

Have a problem? Hope is there
Even if no one cares
Hope is something that keeps you going
Through all the pain that you are knowing

Hope will help you get through
So many things you need to do
It gives you strength throughout the day
And makes you feel better in some way

When you have hope there is a future
You will get there I am sure
Hope is what you have to live
Hope is what makes you give

Hope will take you through your life
Hope will help you make it right
If you had no hope, you see
What a poor soul you would be
---fem

"For I know the plans I have for you," declares the Lord, "Plans to prosper you and not to harm you, Plans to give you hope and a future".
Jeremiah 29:11

MY BELIEFS

Am I Worthy?

Lord, am I worthy?
Why did You pick me?
So many people on this earth
But You have chosen me from birth

I cannot help but wonder
On this question I ponder
Why I am the lucky one
Who will see Christ, Your Son

What was the reason You chose me
This is an answer I cannot see
People who never heard of you
Will they go to Heaven too?

Please do not get me wrong
I am happy You chose me among
The people who will go to heaven
When their earthly life has ended

This is something I don't understand
But I leave it in Your hands
You know what is best for us all
I only hope that I won't fall

I want to keep my faith strong
I don't want to do anything wrong
That's why I am so glad that You
Have given unconditional love too

No matter what I do or say
You'll forgive and hear me pray
Thanking You for sending Your Son
To give us all salvation

I cannot figure out why
You chose me, so hard I try
But I trust in You alone
I am so glad You call me Your own.
---fem

I wrote the next poem, 'Gone' when I was planning my funeral. I want this poem read at that time.

GONE

When I am dead and gone
You'll need to carry on
Without me you will be
But think of what I see

I see Jesus who gave His life for me
So I could with Him forever be
He gave His life for you too
He showed the love he has for you

I see the Holy Spirit and our Lord
And all the people who came before
I see Dad, Grandpa, relatives and friends
Oh the joy never ends!

The amazing beauty of this place
Is really something to embrace
Please be happy for me
I have no pain at all, you see

I love you, that will never end
I'm waiting for you and will take your hand
When it's your turn to come here
There is absolutely nothing to fear

Know that God will comfort you
In any sadness you're going through
Keep Him in your heart always
So we can be together again someday

Loving you forever and ever!
---fem
Mom/Grandma

THE HOLY TRINITY

Some people don't understand the Trinity
That three in one are Unity
How can one be split into three
And all take care of you and me

It is what a marriage is like to me
Two people united as one in sanctity
Each has their own purpose for what they do
But together they are united too

As in the Holy Trinity they have their roles
Different things to do and know
The husband is also the head
Full of compassion, this should be said

God the Father as the head is full of love
He takes care of you from above
He makes the plans He has for you
And guides your path to see you through

Jesus the Son submits to Him
And does what is asked of Him
Jesus our Savior came down from heaven
He rose from the dead and will come again

The Holy Spirit gives us hope and faith
He submits to the Father like a wife
The wife submits and helps her husband
But united they are a couple then

Three in One how can it be
How can there be a Holy Trinity?
They are united in love
They work together from above

The Sacred, Holy Trinity
All together for you and me
They give us love and our beliefs
Take care of us when in grief

We can't do without all three
The ones who are joined in unity
God the Father, God the Son
God the Holy Spirit, three in one

---fem

REJOICE

Rejoice and be glad
Though you feel sad
Sing praises to Him
Though things look grim

Give God all your problems today
He will take care of them His way
No need to worry or get upset
God will always take care of it

All you need to do is believe
Then the Lord will never leave
He forgives all of your sins
The devil defeated, Jesus lives

God will always take care of you
Despite all the bad things we do
His love is unending for us all
Even if we slip and fall

He watches over us from above
Can't you feel all of His love?
So many signs that He is with you
Think a bit, you'll come up with a few

He deserves all our praise
So let all our voices raise
In thanks for all He has done
Jesus died for us; eternity won

---*fem*

GOD IS GREAT

God is good and so very great
This beautiful world He did create
Look at the flowers and the trees
He has made all of these

He is also there for you
Through your pain and sorrows too
God loves and cares for you
Without His love what would we do

The devil tempts us all the time
Especially when things aren't so fine
We need to know God is always there
He has so much love to share

Through all your struggles whatever they be
He will always be with you and me
His arms you will feel around you
God will always comfort you

Don't worry, don't be anxious
He is there for all of us
Go with God, He'll be with you
He is the One to see you through

Remember your gift of love
Remember your home will be above
The challenges of the world are great
But His promise is one to celebrate

---*fem*

ODDS AND ENDS

These are poems of different events that I experienced. Some are rather frivolous and you may not get a lot out of some of them. I thought I would add them anyway.

FIREFLIES

Fireflies light up the dark
I hear a woodpecker hitting the bark
An orange butterfly flutters its wings
These are all such beautiful things

The clouds above fluffy and light
The sun shining ever so bright
The sight of a baby deer
Everything is so peaceful here

Who would have thought of these
Only God who made them with ease
This wonderful world we see
Was created for you and me

He gave all of this with His love
Our dear Lord from above
He loves us so much He sent His Son
To give salvation to everyone

Thank God for all of these things
And for the eternal life He brings
Praise the Father and the Son
Praise the Holy Spirit - the Three in One
---fem

CLASS REUNION

I am going to my class reunion
Will I recognize anyone?
How many wrinkles will they have
Has their hair turned gray? Mine has

How many can still dance a jig
Or just be able to stand on a leg
Will there be canes, walkers or such
All of this thinking is just too much

I am going to have a good time
With people who are as old as I
And when the night is sadly over
I will have good things to remember
              ---fem

Faye Marks

Illustrated by Ellie Baumgartner

FIREWORKS

We're waiting in anticipation
At this July 4 celebration
It will all be starting soon
We will hear boom, bang, boom!

The fireworks have begun
We are having so much fun
Look, look up to the sky
Everyone releases a sigh

Beautiful colors; red, blue and green
So many glittering shapes we see
What a beautiful sight to behold
Fireworks for me will never grow old

Up, up there they go
Bursting into a beautiful glow
Up to the sky everyone stares
To see the beauty bursting in air

Then all of a sudden everything stops
No more do you hear any pops
The fireworks finished, no more to see
Now homeward bound with our memories
---fem

FOOTBALL

We're watching the game
I'm so glad I came
We had lots of fun
Seeing who won

Kristi will be having a football party
Where we'll all eat things not so hearty
It will be a fantastic time for sure
No matter who wins, but I hope it's LaFleur

---fem

PORTA-POTTY

When I was in the Porta-Potty
It wasn't because I was naughty
It was hot and stuffy in there
It sure could have used a little more air

When I got out I felt a breeze
I could breathe with a lot more ease
What a good thing for me to be
Out of that 'ole Porta-Potty
---fem

Enjoying their memory bears and pillow made from their grandfather's clothing.

ABOUT THE AUTHOR

Faye Marks lives in a small town in Wisconsin. She leads a simple life and wouldn't have it any other way. She was blessed with a husband for 49 years (he passed away in 2021) and has a love for farming because of him. They worked side by side throughout their married life. She is also blessed with four adult children and their own children. She is a very proud mom and grandma.

She began composing poems for her children and grandchildren, marking special occasions such as birthdays and high school and college graduations. She even surprised her youngest daughter by reading a poem as a prayer during her wedding ceremony.

She has lived with depression for most of her adult life and began writing poems as a way to express her innermost feelings. Her poems reflect her experiences and struggles with depression. After her husband's death, she also wrote poems about the grief she continues to experience. "It is the hardest thing I've ever had to go through," she says. Three years later, she is still struggling to let go, torn between not wanting to forget and wanting to move on with her life without him. She believes that she wouldn't be the person she is today if it weren't for him.

God has been a constant presence in her life for as long as she can remember. She doesn't always understand His actions or reasons, but she believes that everything He does ultimately leads to good. She feels that He has answered many of her prayers and protected her from things she didn't even realize at the time. These thoughts and feelings are reflected in her book. She wants to emphasize that these are her personal beliefs and not meant to offend anyone. They are an integral part of her life, along with experiences such as depression and grief, which she has also written about.

The publishing of her first book, *"Poems from the Heart,"* was a direct result of all her feelings. In sharing her poems, she hopes to help others who are struggling. She also began sewing stuffed "memory bears" made from the clothes of a loved one who has passed away, so there is something tangible to remember them by. This has grown into making pillows, wall hangings, memory dogs, and she is also experimenting with making memory cows and pigs. As this brings comfort to those she makes them for, it also makes her feel good to see their eyes light up when they recognize the fabrics that were used to make them.

Her new book, *"Whispers of the Heart,"* is a continuation of her first book. It contains more poems that she has written since publishing her first book. She continues to write poems as they help to relieve some of the pain, anxiety, and stress she experiences.

You will find these poems inspiring, encouraging, and full of hope. Most importantly, the poet wants you to know that you are not alone in what you are going through. She encourages you to share them with friends and family so that they, too, do not feel alone. "Helping others is the best feeling. You give, but you also receive."

Beacon of Hope Award for Poetic Justice and Mental Health Awareness Excellence

Awarded to Faye Marks at the Beacon of Hope and Social Change Mission forum in New York City, August 2024.

ACKNOWLEDGEMENTS

I want to express my gratitude to Nadene Joy for writing the Foreword for this book. I am thankful for her continuous enthusiasm and encouragement throughout the process of creating both books. She is a remarkable individual, and I feel fortunate to have her in my life.

Thank you to Kelly Markey and Dave Markey for their assistance and support throughout the creation of this book. They are both incredibly talented individuals.

I am grateful to my daughter, Bobbi for allowing me to include a couple of her beautiful poems in my book. Her unique talents in poetry and songwriting have added a special touch to this book.

I would like to express my gratitude to the illustrators who contributed to my book. I am particularly proud of the artwork created by my granddaughters, Lizzie, Addie and Karlie. I would also like to extend my thanks to Ellie Baumgartner, the 10-year-old daughter of a friend, for the wonderful fireworks picture. I thoroughly enjoyed watching the fireworks with her this year.

I want to express my heartfelt thanks to my family, friends, and all who have supported and helped me along this amazing journey. Their collective efforts have been instrumental in bringing this book to life.

"Each one should use whatever gift he has received. To serve others, faithfully administering God's Grace in its various forms." 1 Peter 4:10

www.ingramcontent.com/pod-product-compliance
Lightning Source LLC
Chambersburg PA
CBHW040632100526
44585CB00030B/130